DE HAVILLAND MOTHS

A FAMILY ALBUM

Ron Smith

CONTENTS

FOREWORD

This is an informal look at a delightful Moth-series of 1920s and 1930s single-engine aircraft designed and built by the de Havilland Aircraft Company, based initially at their Stag Lane factory and airfield in North London and later at Hatfield, Hertfordshire. I find this to be a very pleasant reminder of my own 50-year association with these very practical small aircraft, many of which I have flown over the years. And several of which I have flown with Ron.

We both worked together at the British Aerospace headquarters at Farnborough, and found quite a few excuses to get airborne in the Moths in the local area. Ron himself is a very experienced and capable engineer and pilot, and one flight we completed together in a Hornet Moth in 1994 points also to his excellent navigation capability. Ron navigated us in G-AELO round an eight-hour 55 minute set of flights to win that year's Pooleys / Tiger Club "Dawn to Dusk" International Flying Competition. Ron managed to steer us to and then photograph virtually all the current and earlier aircraft factories in England on a route with more than forty turning points, and that was without GPS assistance!

I hope you will find this book a delightful reminder of some of the nicest aircraft produced by the famous de Havilland Aircraft Company, many of which are still airworthy more than eighty years after leaving the factory.

Colin Dodds, MRAES

ABOUT THE AUTHOR

Dr Ron Smith is an aeronautical engineer, aircraft owner and pilot. His professional career includes 15 years at Westland Helicopters (ten years as Head of Future Projects), and 21 years at British Aerospace/BAE SYSTEMS. He is now retired.

Dr Smith has played an active part in the profession of Aeronautics, as a past Chairman of the Royal Aeronautical Society (RAeS) Rotorcraft Committee and a past member of the RAeS Council. He is a current member of the RAeS Historical Group Committee.

The author is a member of the following organisations and societies: Royal Aeronautical Society (Fellow), Institute of Physics (Member), Light Aircraft Association (LAA), Vintage Aircraft Club, and the De Havilland Moth Club.

With more than 35 years experience as a private pilot and more than 30 years as an aircraft owner, his other interests include aircraft photography and writing aviation books. His previous works include the five volume *British Built Aircraft* series; *Cessna 172: A Pocket History*; and *Piper Cherokee: A Family History*. He has written an aviation memoir *Two Up* with his identical twin brother Jim.

INTRODUCTION

This volume presents a photo album of the De Havilland Moth family from the Cirrus Moth through to the Hornet Moth and Moth Minor. The Moth was of fundamental importance to the development of the practical and affordable light aeroplane. The type first flew in February 1925 and was immediately successful in its own right, and in encouraging other companies to enter this marketplace. By mid-1930, of 288 private aircraft registered in the UK, 172 (60%) were Moths; only three other types reached double figures, one of these being De Havilland's own Puss Moth.

For many people, the progenitor of the Moth was the De Havilland DH51. This three seat tourer was powered by the 120 hp Airdisco V8 engine, but proved too expensive to buy and operate, with only three being built. Recognising this, De Havilland designed a smaller single bay biplane around the 60 hp ADC Cirrus four cylinder in-line engine. The engine itself had been created by Frank Halford of Airdisco effectively by using one bank of the earlier Airdisco V-8. Thus was born the DH60 Cirrus Moth.

De Havilland DH51 'Miss Kenya' progenitor of the Moth, flying at the Shuttleworth Trust, Old Warden, Bedfordshire

Progressive development of the airframe and engine resulted in the Gipsy Moth, Moth Major, Tiger Moth and Fox Moth, each of which was built in large numbers. Monoplanes within the family included the closely-related Puss Moth and Leopard Moth and the low wing Moth Minor. The biplane Hornet Moth provided a comfortable enclosed cabin biplane touring aircraft.

The less familiar Moth types, which are also covered here are the DH61 Giant Moth commercial biplane; the DH71 Tiger Moth monoplane, used for high speed testing of the Gipsy engine; the DH75 Hawk Moth commercial monoplane; and the one-off DH81 Swallow Moth low wing monoplane.

The majority of the photographs presented are from the author's own collection. Photographs from other sources are individually credited. The author is an ex-employee of BAE Systems and works part-time with the BAE Systems Heritage Group. Grateful acknowledgement is given for permission to use a number of images of the less well-known types, taken from the BAE Systems archive at Farnborough. Where these images originate from third parties, this is also indicated, where the source is known. A number of the photographs were taken at the De Havilland Moth Club Rally at Woburn Abbey and membership of this organisation is highly recommended for all with an interest in this delightful family of aircraft.

The technical origin of the Moth is described above. It is worth, however, contemplating how the family came to be so named. Within the BAE Systems archive is held a book, entitled 'British Moths'. This was written by JW Tutt and was published in 1896 by George Routledge and Sons.

For its significance in this context, it is only necessary to refer to the inscription contained within, which is reproduced here. The book was given to Geoffrey de Havilland by his mother on his 15th birthday on 27 July 1897. This is, perhaps, the true origin of the De Havilland Moth family.

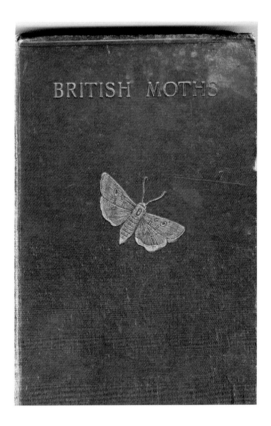

The book British Moths by JW Tutt from the BAE Systems Heritage archive. Perhaps this is the true origin of the De Havilland Moth family?   *BAE SYSTEMS*

DE HAVILLAND DH60 CIRRUS MOTH (AND DH60X HERMES MOTH)

FIRST FLIGHT – FEBRUARY 1925

G-EBLV is the 8th Cirrus Moth built. It was built in 1925 and is owned by BAE Systems, and is based at Old Warden. It was photographed displaying there in 2003

The prototype DH60 Moth G-EBKT flew for the first time at Stag Lane on 22 February 1925. The main variants were the Cirrus and Hermes Moth (described here) and the DH60G Gipsy Moth (described separately). The Moth was immediately successful and was, effectively, the world's first affordable, practical and safe light aeroplane. The type benefited from its selection to equip a number of officially supported flying clubs.

The practicality of the design was ably demonstrated by a number of long distance flights, racing successes and altitude records. Notable flights were made by Cobham (London to Zurich and back in a day); T Neville Stack (to India) and Lady Bailey (to and from South Africa); and RR Bentley (to Cape Town and back). From 1926 onward, the 80hp Cirrus II was fitted to production machines, these being known as Cirrus II Moths. A small number of aircraft, including six for the RAF were fitted with the 75 hp Genet I radial engine.

From 1928, production switched to the DH60X, distinguished by a spilt axle undercarriage (with struts forming an X between the undercarriage legs), fitted with the 90 hp Cirrus II (although some were fitted with the 105 hp Cirrus Hermes I). The Cirrus Moth was widely exported with licence manufacture in Australia and Finland. The type was succeeded in production by the DH60G Gipsy Moth, by which time some 403 had been built, the majority being DH60X (Cirrus II and Hermes) Moths.

There are relatively few original Cirrus Moths still flying. 1928 DH60X Hermes Moth G-EBWD was Richard Shuttleworth's personal aircraft and forms part of The Shuttleworth Trust collection at Old Warden Bedfordshire

The immaculate condition of BAE Systems' 1925 Cirrus Moth G-EBLV is evident in this photograph taken in October 2014

G-EBWD was originally built as a Cirrus II-powered DH60X. This photograph shows the split undercarriage with its characteristic X struts. This split undercarriage was used on all later models of the Moth.

An air-to-air photograph of the De Havilland Cirrus Moth G-EBLV, which was rebuilt at Hatfield and remains in the ownership of BAE Systems.
BAE SYSTEMS

G-EBWD parked in the summer sun at Old Warden. The Handley Page automatic slat is visible at the outboard leading edge of the starboard wing. The exhaust on the starboard side is a distinguishing feature from the Gipsy Moth.

VH-UAU was built for the RAAF in 1928 as a Cirrus II DH60X seaplane. It has been converted to landplane configuration with a fixed cross axle, rather than a split axle undercarriage. It is displayed in the Powerhouse Museum, Sydney, NSW and is one of very few Cirrus Moths displayed in museums.

J8816 is the first of six Genet Moths supplied to the RAF – the small diameter of the Genet engine is apparent.
Flight International via BAE Systems

The DH60X Hermes Moth G-EBWD landing at Old Warden. The starboard exhaust and exposed cylinders are distinctive recognition features of the Cirrus Moth series.

DE HAVILLAND DH60G GIPSY MOTH AND DH60M
FIRST FLIGHT – JULY 1928

Newly restored 1930 Gipsy Moth G-AAJT was winner of the Concours at the 2014 Moth Club Rally at Woburn Abbey

The DH60G was an improved version of the Cirrus Moth, making use of the 100hp de Havilland Gipsy I engine. Later production models were also fitted with the 105 hp Cirrus Hermes, or the 120hp Gipsy II engine. Parallel production took place of a metal tube fuselage version, the DH60M, the two variants being built in similar numbers. Production switched from the Cirrus Moth to the Gipsy Moth in late 1928.

The type won the 1928 King's Cup Air Race and, shortly thereafter, Geoffrey de Havilland set an altitude record of 21,000 ft, flying G-AAAA. The type is, however, best known for long-distance flights, including by such famous pilots as Amy Johnson (London to Australia in G-AAAH 'Jason', preserved in the Science Museum, London), Francis Chichester (London to Australia and his famous flight across the Tasman Sea from New Zealand to Australia), Jim Mollison (Australia to England), John Grierson (flights to Lahore, to Moscow and to Baghdad), CWA Scott (London to Australia) among many others.

Some 595 examples of the DH60G were built at Stag Lane, with a further 80 aircraft built under licence in France, the United States and Australia. Although less well-known, some the DH60M was produced in similar numbers (~550) to the DH60G, along with some 63 DH60T Moth Trainer, which was a military training version of the DH60M. The DH60M was also built in significant numbers in Canada (35), the United States (161) and Norway (10). In October 2014, some 22 DH60G and DH60M appeared on the UK civil register.

G-AANV is a 1931 DH60M built by Morane Saulnier in France. It was previously registered HB-OBU and was photographed at Compton Abbas, Wiltshire.

1930 DH60G Gipsy Moth G-ABEV photographed at Henstridge, Somerset. This aircraft previously operated in the US as N4203E.

G-AADR is a DH60GM Moth, with metal fuselage structure and fabric covering, rather than the plywood covering of the DH60G. This aircraft was built in 1929 by the Moth Aircraft Corporation as NC939M and is seen at Brickhouse Farm airstrip, near Bristol.

G-AAMY is a DH60GM Moth, with metal fuselage structure and fabric covering. This aircraft starred in the film *Out of Africa* and was built in 1929 by the Moth Aircraft Corporation as NC585M and is seen at the Badminton House airstrip. Unusually, this American-built aircraft has its exhaust on the starboard side.

G-AAHI is a 1929 DH60G Gipsy Moth photographed at the 2014 DH Moth Club Rally at Woburn Abbey. The fairing over the engine cylinders distinguishes the type from the earlier Cirrus Moth. This aircraft was built as a Moth Coupé and has been rebuilt using parts of G-AAWO.

G-AAJT landing at the 2014 Moth Club Rally at Woburn Abbey. The Handley Page automatic slats on the upper wing leading edge can clearly be seen.

G-AANF is a DH60GM Moth, and was built in 1929 by the Moth Aircraft Corporation as NC237K (and later N298M) and is seen at the Badminton House airstrip. This aircraft, like G-AAMY, has its exhaust on the starboard side. It is now operating in New Zealand.

VH-UAE was originally built in 1925 as a Cirrus Moth and subsequently converted to DH60X configuration. It was further modified to a DH60G Gipsy Moth with a Gipsy I (and later Gipsy II) engine. This is Australia's oldest airworthy aircraft. *Jim Smith*

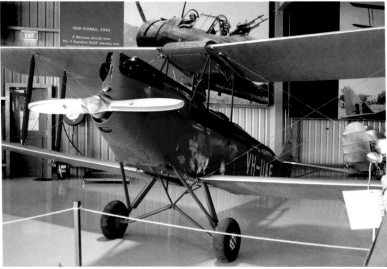

1930 DH60G Gipsy Moth G-AAWO, seen at Henstridge, Somerset in the company of Tiger Moth G-APCC.

G-AAHY is a 1929 DH60M, built in the UK and exported to Switzerland as HB-AFR. It subsequently returned to the UK in 1983. It was photographed with wings folded at Cranfield, Bedfordshire.

1930 DH60G G-AAMZ on take-off from Woburn Abbey in 1995. Previously on the Spanish register as M-CHAA and later as EC-ABX, it has subsequently been exported to the US as N60MZ.

Morane Saulnier-built DH60M G-AANV
photographed at Cranfield, Bedfordshire.

1930 Gipsy Moth G-ABAG
photographed at Thruxton, Hampshire
in 1974. This aircraft has been based in
the UK since new and was restored to
flying condition in 1974.

1933 DH60G G-ATBL climbs away at Sywell, Northamptonshire. This aircraft was exported new to Switzerland as CH-353, later HB-OBA. It returned to the UK in 1965.

MOTH AIRCRAFT CORPORATION
LOWELL MASS
LICENSEE: THE DE HAVILLAND AIRCRAFT CO., LTD.

The logo of the Moth Aircraft Corporation reproduced on the side of DH60M G-AAMY

French-built DH60M G-AANV shortly before touchdown at Henstridge, Somerset.

1930 US-built DH60M G-AAMX on display in 2004 in the Milestones of Flight Gallery at the RAF Museum, Hendon in a particularly attractive colour-scheme.

Gipsy Moth G-AADV equipped with a single central amphibious float.
Flight International photograph via BAE SYSTEMS

DH60M G-AANF taxying at Badminton House airstrip

DH60M G-AAMY taking-off at the airstrip at Badminton House.

G-AAAH 'Jason' is possibly the most famous Gipsy Moth, having been used for long-distance flights by Amy Johnson, including a record-breaking solo flight from England to Australia in May 1930. Built in 1928, the aircraft ceased to be flown after the end of 1930, being donated to the Science Museum, South Kensington, at the end of the following year. It was photographed there in April 2014.

DE HAVILLAND DH60GIII MOTH AND MOTH MAJOR

FIRST FLIGHT – MARCH 1932

1934 DH60GIII Moth Major G-ACNS photographed at Abingdon, Oxfordshire. The type is essentially a DH60 Moth with an inverted Gipsy III or Gipsy Major engine. The lack of wing stagger is an identifying feature compared with the Tiger Moth.

The DH60GIII Moth used the de Havilland Gipsy III inverted engine, which allowed a cleaner, lower engine installation. The prototype DH60GIII G-ABUI flew for the first time in March 1932, An improved version of this engine, the Gipsy IIIA, was produced in large quantities as the 130hp Gipsy Major, which powered many types of light aircraft from the Puss Moth to the Chipmunk (with a Gipsy Major Mk10). Powered by this engine, the type became known as the Moth Major.

A total of 154 DH60GIII aircraft were built with either the Gipsy III or Gipsy Major engine; of these, more than half were exported world-wide. Fifty-seven of the total were Gipsy III Moths, the remainder being Moth Majors, ninety-six of which were built at Stag Lane, with one further example built by the de Havilland Technical School.

Although not as famous for long distance flying as the Gipsy Moth, flights made by DH60GIII included Lisbon to Goa; Lympne to Darwin; Calcutta to Leeming, Yorkshire; and New Delhi to Ceylon and back.

1932 DH60GIII in single seat configuration with a faired pilot's headrest, photographed at Abingdon, Oxfordshire.

DH60GIII EE1-89 (previously 30-89, later EC-AFQ) on display at the Spanish Air Force Museum at Cuatro Vientos, Madrid.

Single seat DH60GIII G-ABZB at Abingdon, Oxfordshire. This aircraft was previously registered in Sweden as SE-AIA.

DE HAVILLAND DH61 GIANT MOTH
FIRST FLIGHT – DECEMBER 1927

The second DH61 G-CAJT under test on floats in 1928 at Rochester.
Flight International photograph via BAE SYSTEMS

The first prototype DH61 (G-EBTL) flew in December 1927 and was named 'Canberra', being intended for use in Australia. It was powered by a 500 hp Bristol Jupiter VI engine but the majority of the production machines used the 500 hp Jupiter XI. The DH61 accommodated 6 to 8 passengers in a glazed and enclosed cabin in the centre of the fuselage, with the pilot seated in an open cockpit to the rear. The 2nd and 3rd aircraft (G-CAJT & G-CAPG) were tested at Rochester in 1928 on Shorts-built floats to evaluate their seaplane operational capability.

In total 10 aircraft were built, 7 of which were exported to Australia and Canada and 2 of these aircraft (G-AUJB Apollo and G-AUJC Diana) were the first Qantas aircraft to be equipped with toilets. In 1935 however they were retired because of the unreliability of the Bristol Jupiter XI engines. One aircraft was used by in the UK by the Daily Mail for rapid news gathering and was equipped with a dark room that could be used in flight to process film negatives. It also carried a motorcycle so that its reporters could be as mobile as possible on arrival at their destination. The aircraft was later sold to the National Flying Service before being acquired by Western Australian Airlines in 1931.

Sir Alan Cobham was notable for his exploits in the DH61 (G-AAEV) as part of his 21 week Tour of Britain to promote aviation in 1929. During the tour, Cobham flew 60,000 miles, visited 110 towns and carried 40,000 passengers including 10,000 schoolchildren experiencing their first flights. This aircraft was fitted with an Armstrong Siddeley Jaguar VIC engine and configured for ten passengers to maximise the potential for passenger flying.

An unregistered DH61 Giant Moth at Stag Lane.   *BAE SYSTEMS*

The prototype DH61 Giant Moth G-EBTL
Canberra photographed at Stag Lane.
Flight International photograph via BAE SYSTEMS

A side view of the prototype DH61 Giant Moth.
Flight International photograph via BAE SYSTEMS

A full size replica of QANTAS DH61 VH-UJB / G-AUJB Apollo on display at Brisbane Airport. This replica is now displayed at the QANTAS Founders Museum at Longreach, Queensland.

DE HAVILLAND DH71 TIGER MOTH

FIRST FLIGHT – JUNE 1927

The first DH71 G-EBQU at the RAF Display, Hendon on 30 June 1928.
Via BAE SYSTEMS

The DH71 was a small and clean low wing monoplane intended for racing and for engine development. Produced as a private venture, its slim fuselage was tailored to just accommodate its slim pilot, Hubert Broad.

Two aircraft were built, G-EBQU powered initially by an ADC Cirrus II, but then fitted with an experimental 130 hp Gipsy engine, and G-EBRV, powered by the 85 hp ADC Cirrus II. Both aircraft received Certificates of Airworthiness in July 1927. The appearance of the DH71 caused something of a sensation; it was probably the first British civil aircraft to be designed specifically for air racing.

G-EBQU was used to set a closed circuit speed record of 186.4 mph on 24 August 1927, followed by an altitude record for its class of 19,191 ft five days later. This aircraft was sold to Australia in 1930, where it was destroyed in an accident in September of the same year.

G-EBRV flew in the 1927 King's Cup Air Race. Although it retired early, Penrose reports in British Aviation: The Adventuring Years that it achieved a speed of 162 mph on the first 26 mile lap, beating its handicap speed by nearly 48 mph. G-EBRV was retained and preserved by the manufacturers, but was destroyed at Hatfield by enemy bombing during the Second World War.

This discussion group around the first DH71
demonstrates both its small size and the
confined nature of the cockpit.
BAE SYSTEMS

The first DH71 landing at Stag Lane in 1927.
Flight International photograph via BAE SYSTEMS

DE HAVILLAND DH75 AND DH75A HAWK MOTH
FIRST FLIGHT – DECEMBER 1928

BAE SYSTEMS

DH75 Hawk Moth prototype G-EBVV at Stag Lane with DH Ghost engine.
BAE SYSTEMS

Frank Halford designed the DH Ghost engine by mating two Gipsy I engines in a common crankcase to produce a 198 hp V-8 engine. The DH75 prototype G-EBVV was designed around this new engine and flew for the first time on 7 December 1928. It was a strut-braced high wing monoplane with a welded steel fuselage and a somewhat ungainly undercarriage arrangement, reminiscent of that adopted by a number of similar American aircraft of the same period. The wing planform was very similar to that adopted for the later DH80 Puss Moth.

It was immediately apparent that the type was underpowered, so it was redesigned as the DH75A. This featured increased wing span and chord and was powered by the 240 hp Armstrong Siddeley Lynx engine. Three aircraft were ordered by the Canadian Government. One aircraft was used as a demonstrator in Australia, leading to the export of an additional example to that market.

One DH75A was entered in the 1930 King's Cup Air race, being placed seventh at an average speed of 126.2 mph.

A final unregistered prototype was constructed in May 1930 as the DH75B, fitted with a 300 hp Wright Whirlwind engine. In total, only eight aircraft were completed, comprising the prototype DH75, six DH75A and the single DH75B.

Ski-equipped DH75A Hawk Moth G-AAFW (later G-CYVD) in Canada in the winter of 1929.
BAE SYSTEMS

DH75A Hawk Moth 'VL' of the Canadian Government (G-CYVL). The steps provided for crew and passenger access are quite prominent.
BAE SYSTEMS

Tests of a DH75A on floats (believed to be G-AAFX).   *BAE SYSTEMS*

DE HAVILLAND DH80A PUSS MOTH

FIRST FLIGHT – SEPTEMBER 1929

The much-travelled Puss Moth G-AAZP landing at the 2014 Moth Club Rally at Woburn Abbey.

The prototype DH80 Puss Moth E-1 / G-AAHZ flew for the first time on 9 September 1929. This one-off aircraft had a flat-sided wooden fuselage, production aircraft, the DH80A, having a fabric-covered steel tube fuselage construction.

The Puss Moth was a high wing two seat light aircraft offering long range and cabin comfort. The seating arrangement allowed the carriage of a second passenger when desired. The wings could be folded back to reduce hangar space, a common feature of a number of light aircraft of the era. The type was immediately successful, achieving sales to private owners world-wide. In addition to the prototype, a total of 259 aircraft were manufactured at Stag Lane, with a further 25 constructed by de Havilland Aircraft of Canada Ltd

In the 1930s, the Puss Moth became a preferred mount for long-distance record-breaking pilots, the type being flown by famous names such as HJ 'Bert' Hinkler, CJ Melrose, the Master of Semphill, Jim and Amy Mollison (Amy Johnson) and others. Their flights ranged from London across the Atlantic and to South Africa; India; Japan; and Brazil.

A number of early production aircraft were lost in flying accidents, these being ultimately traced to wing flutter. The fleet were then modified with an additional bracing strut running from the front wing strut to the wing rear attachment point; a larger rudder was also fitted.

1930 Puss Moth VH-UQB (previously G-ABDW) is displayed at the Scottish Museum of Flight at East Fortune. The undercarriage strut attached at the wing root is a distinguishing feature from the Leopard Moth, where it attaches to the rear upper engine mount.

1931 Puss Moth G-AEOA was originally delivered to Yugoslavia, becoming YU-PAX. It returned to the UK pre-war and was impressed as ES921. It was photographed at Thruxton, Hampshire in the early 1970s, when owned by Dr John Urmston.

G-AAZP photographed at Old Warden. The flap-like segments at the inboard trailing edge fold forwards and upwards to allow the wings to be folded to the rear.

The immaculate spat-equipped 1931 Puss Moth G-ABLS, photographed at Old Warden in October 2014.

This view of G-ABLS on take-off emphasises the clean lines of the Puss Moth.

Dr Urmston's Puss Moth G-AEOA photographed at Thruxton, Hampshire.

1930 DH80A Puss Moth G-ABBS photographed in the Prince of Wales' colours. Unusually, this aircraft is equipped with Handley Page automatic slats. It was later operated in Iraq as YI-ABB.
BAE SYSTEMS

G-AAZP at the 2014 Moth Club Rally at Woburn Abbey. It operated in Egypt as SU-AAC, and later in India. It returned to the UK and was impressed during the war as HL537. In 1984, it was flown by Tim Williams and Henry Labouchere from Mildenhall to Melbourne to celebrate the 50th Anniversary of the 1934 MacRobertson Air Race.

Puss Moth G-AAZP displays at Woburn Abbey. The wing planform with its outboard taper and rounded tips is another distinguishing feature from the DH85 Leopard Moth, which features a straight tapered and slightly swept back planform.

DE HAVILLAND DH81 SWALLOW MOTH
FIRST FLIGHT AUGUST 1931

The DH81 Swallow Moth stands uniquely among the Moth family as the only model that existed solely as a single prototype. This two seat low wing monoplane was powered by an 80hp Gipsy IV engine, the design intent being to create a clean, lower-powered, two seat aircraft that would offer high performance, but be relatively cheap to own and operate.

The Swallow Moth was first flown on 21 August 1931 with open cockpits. Testing showed that these were rather draughty at speed; also, there were some directional handling issues. After testing in autumn 1931, the type was modified as the DH81A with an enclosed hinged cockpit cover and modified fin and rudder. In this form, the aircraft was reported to have achieved a maximum speed of 129 mph, which was extremely good for an aircraft with only an 80 hp engine. Flight testing continued until early February 1932, after which the aircraft was withdrawn from use. The Swallow Moth concept was revived in the DH94 Moth Minor, which was also built with either open, or enclosed, cockpits. Ord-Hume in British Light Aeroplanes – Their Evolution, Development and Perfection 1920 – 1940 indicates that elements of the DH81 prototype, including its Gipsy IV engine may have been re-used in the prototype Moth Minor.

The design also introduced an undercarriage arrangement with the main struts attached to the top longerons immediately aft of the engine bulkhead – a configuration that was re-used on the DH85 Leopard Moth and DH87 Hornet Moth.

The only known photograph of the Swallow Moth (in its DH81A configuration).
Alec Davis via BAE SYSTEMS

DE HAVILLAND DH82A TIGER MOTH AND QUEEN BEE

FIRST FLIGHT – OCTOBER 1931

Left: The classic Tiger Moth cockpit, photographed at Henstridge, Somerset.
Above: Morris Motors-built XL716 / G-AOIL takes off from Compton Abbas.

The prototype DH82 Tiger Moth E-6 (later G-ABRC) flew for the first time on 26 October 1931. Designed from the outset for the training role, the Tiger Moth was developed from the earlier DH60T Moth Trainer by adoption of the inverted Gipsy III engine and a modified centre section to allow the front seat occupant (the instructor) an easier escape in emergencies.

This was achieved by moving the centre section forward of the front cockpit. Wing sweep was then required to restore balance around the centre of gravity, together with increased lower wing dihedral to improve tip clearance. These features distinguish the Tiger Moth from the Moth or Moth Major. Introduction of the Gipsy Major resulted in a change of designation to DH82A. The Tiger Moth rapidly became the standard trainer for civilian and RAF use and was widely exported.

Production numbers are somewhat uncertain with nearly 5,500 built in the UK from a total of some 8,800. Outside the UK, production was undertaken in De Havilland factories in Australia, Canada and New Zealand, together with licence production in Portugal, Norway and Sweden. An additional 420 aircraft were built as Queen Bee target drones, 320 being built at Hatfield and 60 by Scottish Aviation in Glasgow. Large numbers of UK aircraft were built by Morris Motors Ltd, freeing up capacity at Hatfield for construction of the Mosquito. Canadian aircraft (designated DH82C) feature a 145 hp Gipsy Major 1C, cockpit enclosure, tailwheel replacing tail skid, and metal interplane struts.

Restored 1939 Tiger Moth R5246 / G-AMIV flying over the Dorset countryside in May 2011. This aircraft was subsequently exported to Germany as D-EDAH. It was photographed from the author's Jodel D150 Mascaret.

1939 DH82A G-AHMN / N6985 was one of a pair flown by the author from their then home base of Compton Abbas, Wiltshire, in the 1980s.

1941 DH82A T6953 / G-ANNI climbs away from Compton Abbas, Wiltshire in April 2011.

1945 Tiger Moth F-BGDD (previously PG626) being prepared at Biggin Hill, Kent to enter the British register as G-AXXE. This aircraft was sold to Germany as D-EOPR, but crashed on its delivery flight in 1975.
Jim Smith

R5246 '40' nearing completion of its restoration at Henstridge, Somerset. This was the first of six superlative Tiger Moth rebuilds to completed there by Kevin Crumplin.

1940 Tiger Moth XL716 / G-AOIL taxying at its then home base of Compton Abbas, Wiltshire in October 2010.

A17-375 / VH-AKE is a 1941 De Havilland Australia-built example, seen taxying at Echuca, VIC, in April 2013.

This chocolate and pale blue Tiger Moth is G-EMSY, which was built by Morris Motors in 1940. It was previously registered T7356; E-6; D-EDUM; G-ASPZ; and D-EMSY. It was photographed at its home vase of Old Sarum, Wiltshire in July 2011.

VH-AZF (A17-357) was built by De Havilland Australia in 1941 and displays the classic Tiger Moth planform with swept, staggered wings as it flies over Echuca, VIC in April 2013.

The restored three aircraft fleet of Tiger Moth Training, photographed at their Henstridge base at Easter 2014.

Australian-built Tiger Moth VH-AZF taxying at Echuca, VIC. This aircraft is equipped with a tail wheel, unlike most British aircraft, which are fitted with tailskids (and no brakes).

In October 2014, there were no less than 187 Tiger Moths listed on the Australian register. This is A17-673 / VH-CCD, built in Australia in 1942. Its prior identities are DX780; and VH-RNP. This aircraft was photographed at the Australian Antique Aeroplane Association National Fly-in at Echuca, VIC in April 2013.

Another Australian-built Tiger Moth at the AAAA 2013 National Fly-in. This is VH-NWM / A17-227, which was built in 1941. In superb condition, this aircraft is based at Mildura, NSW.

1940 Morris Motors-built Tiger Moth G-EMSY reflects the afternoon sun whilst taking-off from Compton Abbas, Wiltshire in October 2010.

1940 Morris Motors-built Tiger Moth G-AOBX (previously T7187) seen taking off from Old Warden, Bedfordshire in October 2014.

An atmospheric photograph of 1939 Tiger Moth R5246 '40', seen to the south of Henstridge in a photograph that could almost have been taken in the 1940s.

Another lovely air-to-air photograph of restored 1939 Tiger Moth R5246 / G-AMIV flying over the Dorset countryside in May 2011.

N9328 '69' / G-ALWS is one of the Tiger Moth Training fleet photographed at Henstridge Somerset at Easter 2014.

Tiger Club single seat 'Super Tiger' G-AOAA 'The Deacon', with fuel tank moved from the upper centre section to the front cockpit. The photograph dates from the late 1960s and was taken at the Club's then base of Redhill Aerodrome, Surrey. *Jim Smith*

1942 DH82A G-AJHU (previously T7471) about to land at Compton Abbas, Wiltshire in the late 1970s. Note that the automatic slats are deployed as the aircraft begins to flare for its landing.

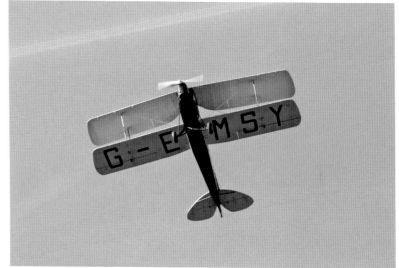

Another classic Tiger Moth plan view as G-EMSY joins overhead to join the circuit at Compton Abbas, Wiltshire in June 2010.

A delightful view of 1935 Tiger Moth G-ADXT as it flies through the overhead to join the circuit at Compton Abbas, Wiltshire in August 2013.

G-ANRX (previously N6550) is preserved in an agricultural configuration at the De Havilland Museum at Salisbury Hall., Hertfordshire.

The late Tony Harold flies the Reading Flying Group 1941 Tiger Moth G-ANFM / T5588 en route between Booker and Blackbushe to a Vintage Aircraft Cub event in 1970. The author had a holiday job with Personal Plane Services at the time and was being flown by Alan Chalkley in his Piper J-3 Cub G-ASPS.

1935 DH82A Tiger Moth G-ADJJ taxying at the 2014 DH Moth Club Rally at Woburn Abbey

1941 Morris Motors-built '41' NM138 / G-ANEW is part of the Tiger Moth Training fleet at Henstridge, Somerset and was photographed in September 2013.

C-FCTN / 5884 is a DH Canada-built DH82C built in 1941. The photograph was taken at the EAA Convention at Oshkosh, Wisconsin in 1980, when the owners were generous enough to give the author a ride in this different Tiger Moth variant.

G-AZZZ is a 1944 Morris Motors built aircraft and was previously registered as NL864 and F-BGJE. It was photographed landing at the 2014 Moth Club Rally at Woburn Abbey, Bedfordshire.

G-APCC was built in 1944 with RAF serial PG640. It is seen here at Henstridge, Somerset, parked next to Gipsy Moth G-AAWO (see the DH60G entry).

N6466 / G-ANKZ is a 1938 aircraft and was photographed landing at the 2014 Moth Club Rally at Woburn Abbey, Bedfordshire.

1940 Morris Motors-built T7404 / G-ANMV photographed at Woburn Abbey in 1995. This is one of two Tiger Moths flown by the author in the 1980s, when it was based at Compton Abbas, Wiltshire.

The author, somewhat lacking in both physical and sartorial elegance, installs himself in T7404 / G-ANMV at Compton Abbas, Wiltshire.

VH-LJM was built by DH Australia in 1942 and has previous identities of A17-561, VH-AUM, VH-FAH, and VH-TSA. This photograph was taken at Avalon, NSW.

VH-APB was built by DH Australia in 1940; its previous identities are A17-116, VH-ATQ and VH-SSB. It was photographed at its base at Camden, NSW.

XL714 / G-AOGR was built by Morris Motors in 1942 as T6099 and is seen here landing at Woburn Abbey in August 2014.

1940 DH82A G-ANEM (previously R5042 and EI-AGN) seen landing at Woburn Abbey during the 2014 DH Moth Club Rally.

G-AOBX (previously T7187) was built in 1940 by Morris Motors and is seen here on the airstrip at Badminton House.

1942 DH82A '91' T6818 / G-ANKT
displaying at The Shuttleworth Trust,
Old Warden, Bedfordshire.

1941 Tiger Moth G-AIDS (previously T6055)
'The Sorcerer' taxying at Woburn Abbey in
August 2014.

Single seat Tiger Moth G-AOAA 'The Deacon' in the Tiger Club hangar at Redhill Aerodrome, Surrey.

1939 DH82A Tiger Moth OO-MEH photographed at Balen Keiheuvel, Belgium in May 1989. This aircraft has had many identities, being previously N9192, A-13 (Dutch), PH-UFB and OO-GEB, and subsequently G-BSTJ and G-DHZF (its current registration).

1941 DH82A T6953 / G-ANNI taxies at the 2014 DH Moth Club Rally at Woburn Abbey in August 2014.

G-AMHF (previously R5144) was built in 1940; it is seen here on the approach to Woburn Abbey in August 2014.

1941 Tiger Moth G-AJHS (previously N6866) photographed at the Badminton House airstrip.

An immaculate 1939 Tiger Moth G-AOJK / R4896 landing at Woburn Abbey in August 2014.

LN-BDM flew 1,000 miles from Oslo to Woburn Abbey for the 2014 Moth Club Rally, It was built in 1942 and was previously registered DE248 and G-ANSC.

G-ALNA photographed at Finmere, Oxfordshire. In the mid-70s, this aircraft was operated by the Wessex Flying Group and hangared on John Fairey's nearby estate. The aircraft was built in 1941 as T6774.

Built in 1943 by Morris Motors as EM729, DH82A Tiger Moth N8233 (previously PH-UAO) is presented in the colours of the Rijksluchtvaartschool (Government Flying School or RLS). It was a visitor to Woburn Abbey in August 2014.

N9328 '69' / G-ALWS is one of Kevin Crumplin's superb Tiger Moth restorations based at Henstridge, Somerset and photographed there in April 2014.

1942 Tiger Moth F-BGCS (previously DF210 and later F-AZTM) was for some years the only Tiger Moth flying in France. It was photographed in the mid-1980s at Brienne le Chateau, France, where it was visiting the RSA Rally.

PH-CSL was built in 1944 as PG712, subsequently serving with the Dutch AF as A-2, and then appearing on the Belgian register as OO-DJU. It was photographed at Woburn Abbey in August 2014.

PH-CSL in an earlier guise with the extended
dorsal fin required by the Dutch authorities.
It was photographed at the KZ Club Rally,
Stauning, Denmark in 1979.

Tiger Moth W--- '18' of No10 Reserve Flying
Training School at Exeter shortly after the
Second World War   *Horace North*

1940 DH82A G-AMHF (previously R5144) takes off in a strong crosswind at Woburn Abbey in August 2014.

The Tiger Club's 1933 Tiger Moth G-ACDC seen at Redhill Aerodrome in the 1960s. For many years, this was the oldest flying Tiger Moth, having been supplanted following the restoration of G-ACDA.

The newly-restored R5246 / G-AMIV seen against the Spring skies of Dorset in May 2011.

1943 Morris Motors-built Tiger Moth G-AHOO (previously EM967 and 6940M) goes around in tricky conditions at Woburn Abbey.

The crew of G-MOTH / DE306 'K2567' demonstrate the somewhat strenuous ground handling technique required. This is a 1942 aircraft in the colours of the first DH82 Tiger Moth. The aircraft also has the larger forward cockpit door appropriate to the early DH82.

1941 DH82A T6953 / G-ANNI after take-off from Compton Abbas, Wiltshire in April 2011.

1935 DH82A Tiger Moth G-ADIA about to touch down at Woburn Abbey in 1995.

G-AHVV was built by Morris Motors in 1943 as EM929. This photograph was taken at Dunkeswell, Devon.

G-ACDA, seen here in the colours of The De Havilland School of Flying, was built in 1933 and is the oldest Tiger Moth still flying.

VH-HKG is an Australian-built Tiger Moth dating from 1941, which has had many previous identities from A17-277 through VH-BNK, VH-PCJ, VH-BCJ and VH-KLH. It is photographed at Geelong, VIC, shortly after being flown by the author.

1942 Australian-built VH-LJM / A17-561 at Avalon, NSW.

A close-up view of 1940 DH82A
Tiger Moth G-AGEG on the airstrip
at Badminton House.

A formation by the Diamond Nine
Moth Club team.

1942 Morris Motors-built G-BAFG (previously EM778 and F-BGEL) taxying at Netherthorpe, South Yorkshire.

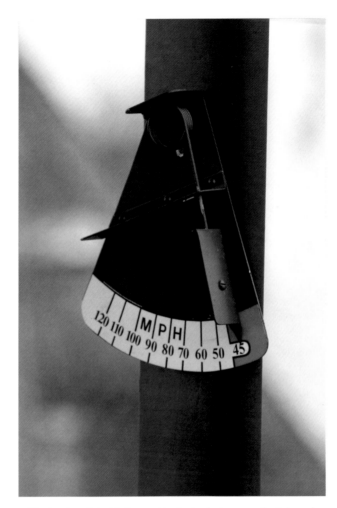

The back-up 'windy' airspeed indicator features on the inboard
face of the front port wing strut of many Tiger Moths.

DE HAVILLAND DH83 FOX MOTH
FIRST FLIGHT – MARCH 1932

1933 DH83 Fox Moth G-ACEJ at Woburn Abbey in August 2014 in the colours of Scottish Motor Traction.

The prototype DH83 Fox Moth G-ABUO flew for the first time in March 1932. The Fox Moth had an open cockpit for its pilot, located well aft on the plywood covered fuselage. Ahead of the pilot and enclosed within the fuselage, there was a small cabin that could seat four passengers. The passengers were provided with side windows and the pilot was provided with a circular glass 'porthole' in the instrument panel so that he could check on the well-being of the passengers. The Fox Moth made use of many Tiger Moth components (including wings, engine mounting and undercarriage).

Despite its limited power, most Fox Moths were delivered to commercial operators including Scottish Motor Traction Ltd (a fleet of eight) and Scottish Air Ferries Ltd (with four). The type was popular for passenger pleasure flights both pre- and post-war. G-ACEJ was used for many years to fly holiday makers from the expansive sands of Southport beach.

A total of 98 were built at Stag Lane, with a further 53 in Canada and two in Australia (for a grand total of 153 aircraft). Canadian examples (DH83C), which were built post-war, used the 145 hp Gipsy Major 1C and were usually fitted with an enclosed sliding cockpit for the pilot.

A particularly notable flight was made by John Grierson in 1934, flying a float-equipped Fox Moth G-ACRX to Ottawa via Iceland and Greenland and continuing from there to New York.

Fox Moth G-ACEJ photographed undergoing maintenance in the Tiger Club hangar at Redhill Aerodrome in the mid-1960s. At this time, the aircraft was painted in all-over silver with Giro Aviation markings.   *Jim Smith*

CF-DJB is a DH83C Fox Moth, built by De Havilland Canada in 1947. This aircraft is on display at The Canadian Aviation & Space Museum at Rockliffe, Ontario. It made its last flight on delivery to the museum in May 1989.   *Jim Smith*

DH83 G-ABUT (later impressed as X9034) waiting for delivery.
Flight International photograph via BAE SYSTEMS

G-AOJH is a 1947 Canadian-built DH83C photographed at the Great Warbirds Spectacular Airshow at Wroughton, Wiltshire, where the author was acting as an assistant judge and as ground crew to DH89 Dragon Rapide G-AEML. This aircraft was initially delivered to Pakistan as AP-ABO.

The cockpit of G-AOJH, showing the brass aircraft limitations plate and the circular window through which the pilot could observe the passengers in the enclosed fuselage cabin.

New Zealand-registered Fox Moth ZK-AEK landed on a beach at South Westland, New Zealand in 1936. This aircraft was originally built as G-ACAJ, being subsequently registered as G-ACDD, OO-ENC, ZK-AEK, and finally VQ-FAT. As G-ACDD it was operated on behalf of the Prince of Wales in appropriate colours and with the coupé canopy seen here. *BAE SYSTEMS*

G-ACEJ shows the general arrangement of the DH83. The wings are unstaggered and the fuselage of increased width to accommodate the passenger cabin. It is, in effect, a modified DH60GIII Moth Major. It was photographed on take-off from Henstridge, Somerset in April 2009.

A ground view of G-ACEJ at Woburn Abbey in August 2014. The passenger cabin with its bulged side windows is shown clearly.

Colin Dodds landing the newly-restored DH83C Fox Moth G-AOJH landing at Woburn Abbey in 1995.

Brian Woodford's 1934 DH83 Fox Moth is presented in the Prince of Wales' colours (originally used on G-ACDD) and is seen at Henstridge, Somerset. The aircraft has subsequently been sold to New Zealand as ZK-ADI. It started life as ZK-ADI, being subsequently registered NZ566, ZK-ASP, N83DH and G-ADHA, before returning to its original identity.

Fox Moth G-ACEJ on short finals to land at Woburn Abbey in August 2014, complete with a lady passenger.

DE HAVILLAND DH85 LEOPARD MOTH

FIRST FLIGHT – MAY 1933

1934 DH85 Leopard Moth G-ACOJ (previously F-AMXP) taking off from Woburn Abbey in 1995.

The prototype DH80 Puss Moth E-1 (later G-ACHD) flew for the first time on 27 May 1933. Unlike the earlier DH80 Puss Moth, the D85 was designed from the outset to carry three occupants and featured a plywood, rather than steel tube fuselage construction. Externally, the two aircraft are similar, although the DH85 undercarriage legs attach at the engine bulkhead, rather than to the forward wing root fitting. The Leopard Moth wing also features straight leading and trailing edges, with the leading edge being gently swept back.

The Leopard Moth was very much an improved Puss Moth, offering the same attractions of long range and cabin comfort. The seating arrangement featured the pilot sat up front, ahead of a rear bench seat accommodating two passenger. The wings could also be folded back to reduce hangar space.

The type was immediately successful, and a total of 132 aircraft were manufactured at Stag Lane and Hatfield. A number of distinguished private owners flew the type, which also conducted dome notable long distance flights including a flight to Australia and back by Ken Waller in March and April 1934. A French aircraft was also flown from Marseilles to Madagascar and back; a Portuguese aircraft also completed a 43,500 mile round trip from Lisbon to Timor and back via the Cape Verde islands.

The prototype Leopard Moth E-1 at Stag Lane; this aircraft was later registered G-ACHD.   *BAE SYSTEMS*

1934 Leopard Moth G-AIYS at Popham, Hampshire showing the folding wings and the undercarriage strut geometry. This aircraft was originally registered in Egypt as SU-ABM and then in Iraq as YI-ABI.

1935 Leopard Moth G-APKH photographed at Booker (High Wycombe) in the early 1970s. This aircraft is a rebuild of two aircraft including G-ACGS which was impressed during the war as AX858. This aircraft was subsequently sold in Switzerland.

Leopard Moth G-APKH in a different colour scheme from that shown previously. The aircraft in the background is Leopard Moth G-AIYS, also in an earlier colour scheme than was shown previously. This photograph was taken at Middle Wallop, Hampshire.

1934 Leopard Moth G-ACUS (previously HB-OXA) seen alongside its sister aircraft G-AIXS, both aircraft belonging to the same owners.

The immaculate Leopard Moth G-AIYS taxying at Woburn Abbey in August 2014.

Leopard Moth G-AIYS on the approach to Popham, Hampshire in July 2014. The straight wing leading and trailing edges are apparent in this photograph.

Leopard Moth G-AIYS seen at Cranfield, Bedfordshire in its maroon colour scheme. The wing folding geometry with the forward folded sections of the inboard trailing edge is clearly visible.

Leopard Moth G-ACOJ taxying at Woburn Abbey in 1995.

Leopard Moth OO-NAD awaiting delivery at Stag Lane. This is one of the early aircraft with a flat-sided fuselage.
Aeroplane photograph via BAE SYSTEMS

The fourth Leopard Moth G-ACHC. This early aircraft has flat fuselage sides and a small fairing at the top of the undercarriage strut.
BAE SYSTEMS

The gleaming Leopard Moth G-AIYS about to touch down at the DH Moth Club Rally at Woburn Abbey in August 2014.

Leopard Moth G-ACUS celebrating the 50th Anniversary of the Vintage Aircraft Club at Popham, Hampshire in July 2014.

1934 Leopard Moth G-ACMN; this aircraft was impressed during the Second World War as X9381.

The bevel gear at the top of the undercarriage strut allows it to be rotated through 90 degrees to act as an air brake. The same arrangement is used on the DH87 Hornet Moth.

Two photographs taken at Goodwood in 1982 of the newly restored DH85 Leopard Moth G-AIYS showing the pilots position and instrument panel and the pilot and passenger seats. Note the DH logo on the rear seat anti-macassars. *Photos: Jeff Bloxham*

DE HAVILLAND DH87 HORNET MOTH

FIRST FLIGHT – MAY 1934

1935 DH87B Hornet Moth G-ADKL departing from Old Warden, Bedfordshire in October 2014. This aircraft was impressed as W5750 during the war, returning to the British register before spending time in France as F-BJCO, before restored to the UK register as G-ADKL.

The prototype DH87 Hornet Moth E-6 (later G-ACTA) flew for the first time on 9 May 1934. The Hornet Moth combined a biplane configuration with the advantages of fully enclosed side-by-side seating. There were clear echoes of the DH85 in respect of the Gipsy Major engine installation. The prototype features slightly tapered wings with a rounded tip shape.

Before production commenced, the wing planform was changed to a high aspect ratio tapered elliptical shape reminiscent of that used by the DH86 Express. In this form, the type was known as the DH87A. The tapered wing was prone to sudden tip stall and this gave rise to operational concerns.

In 1936, G-ADIS appeared having been modified with new square-tipped wings with very slight taper. This became the new production standard, the aircraft then being known as the DH87B. DH87A owners were invited to have the new wings fitted to replace the pointed originals.

A total of 165 Hornet Moths were built, with approximately half of these exported. A number of aircraft operated on either floats or skis in Canada.

1936 DH87B G-ADKW of The London Aeroplane Club flying over Panshanger Aerodrome.   *BAE SYSTEMS*

This fine air-to-air photograph shows the elliptical wing planform of the first DH87A G-ADIS. Like most DH87A, it was retrospectively converted to a DH87B; it was impressed as W9391 and struck off charge in June 1944. *Aeroplane photograph via BAE SYSTEMS*

1936 DH87B G-ADNE 'Ariadne' taking off from Woburn Abbey in 1995.

1936 DH87B Hornet Moth in an elegant and refined green, gold and white colour scheme on the approach to Woburn Abbey in August 2014.

1936 DH87B Hornet Moth G-AELO in the evening light at Little Gransden on 28 July 1994 after the completion of an 8hr 55 min flight around Britain covering 625 miles with more than 40 turning points and three intermediate landings. This was the winning entry in the 1994 Dawn to Dusk Competition, flown by Colin Dodds and researched, planned and navigated by the author.

1937 DH87B VH-UXY photographed at the Australian Antique Aeroplane Association national fly-in at Echuca, VIC in April 2013. This aircraft was originally G-AEZG prior to its export to Australia.

G-AELO at Pocklington, Yorkshire waiting to fly the planned Dawn to Dusk Competition route in July 1994. Early fog in the Vale of York meant a six day wait before setting off for the flight.

DH87B G-ADOT is currently displayed at the DH Museum, Salisbury Hall, Hertfordshire. Wing folding requires the fitting of jury struts at the leading edge of each wing root as can be seen here.

G-ADNE 'Ariadne' photographed at
Biggin Hill, Kent in May 1980.
Jim Smith

1935 DH87B Hornet Moth G-AHBM at
Woburn Abbey in August 2014. This aircraft
was initially delivered to Canada as CF-BFJ.

Hornet Moth G-ADKL prepares to land at Woburn Abbey in August 2014.

DH87B G-AHBL lands in difficult crosswind conditions at Woburn Abbey in August 2014.

G-ADLY in an earlier colour scheme when exhibited at the Southend Air Museum, Essex.

1935 DH87B Hornet Moth G-ADLY with DH83C G-AOJH at Woburn Abbey in 1995.

The blue and white 1935 Hornet Moth
G-ADKK among the gathering of the type
at Woburn Abbey in August 2014.

1936 DH87B G-ADUR photographed
in an attractive green and cream colour
scheme at Greenham Common, Berkshire.

The beautiful G-ADMT makes a 'wheeler' landing in the crosswind at Woburn Abbey.

Hornet Moth G-ADKC was built in 1936 and served with the RAF during the war as X9445. Another member of the Hornet Moth gathering in 2014.

1935 Hornet Moth G-ADKM about to touch down. Note that the undercarriage struts are rotated to the air brake position.

G-AESE lines up with its fellow Hornet Moths at Woburn Abbey in August 2014. This aircraft was impressed as W5775 during the war.

The magnificent condition of G-ADKL is apparent in this photograph taken at the 2014 Moth Club Rally.

G-ADNE makes a wheeler landing in the crosswinds at Woburn Abbey.

G-AELO takes off in the evening light at Henstridge, Somerset in August 2014.

G-AELO photographed at Biggin Hill, Kent in the late 1960s in the blue and yellow colour scheme of Surrey and Kent Flying Club.

DE HAVILLAND DH94 MOTH MINOR

FIRST FLIGHT – JUNE 1937

1939 DH94 Moth Minor Coupé taking off from Middle Wallop, Hampshire.

The prototype DH94 Puss Moth E-4/G-AFRD flew for the first time at Hatfield on 22 June 1937. The Moth Minor was powered by a 90hp Gipsy Minor engine and sat two in tandem open cockpits. Nine aircraft were also fitted with an enclosed cockpit canopy and were known as the Moth Minor Coupé.

The aircraft had a conventional plywood and spruce fuselage, but the high aspect ratio wing was skinned with plywood, like the earlier Comet Racer and Albatross. The wing could be folded from a point outside each undercarriage leg to minimise hangar space requirements. Due to its clean lines, the aircraft was fitted with a perforated airbrake installed between the undercarriage legs.

Following the outbreak of the Second World War, production at Hatfield was abandoned after 73 aircraft had been completed and the manufacturing drawing tools and fixtures passed to De Havilland Australia where at least another 40 aircraft were completed.

Development of the type was somewhat protracted whilst satisfactory spinning characteristics were achieved and this may have contributed to a slow start to production.

An energetic take-off by Moth Minor E-8 at Hatfield, Hertfordshire. This photograph clearly shows the efficient, high aspect ratio wing.
Aeroplane photograph via BAE SYSTEMS

1939 Moth Minor A21-42 (previously VH-ACR, now registered as VN-CZB) photographed at Avalon, VIC. *Jim Smith*

DH94 Moth Minor Coupé photographed at a PFA Rally at Wroughton, Wiltshire.

Open Cockpit Moth Minor G-AFPN photographed at a PFA Rally at Sywell, Northamptonshire.

A fine air-to-air photograph of the 5th Moth Minor G-AZRE, emphasising the attractive lines of the type.   *BAE SYSTEMS*

E-0226 is a Moth Minor experimentally converted to a tricycle under carriage configuration and also has an enclosed rear cockpit.
BAE SYSTEMS

E-6 is an experimental long range single seat Moth Minor with long range tanks installed in the rear cockpit.

Moth Minor Coupé G-AFOJ (previously E-1 and E-0236) photographed in the 1970s in store at Jenkin's Farm, Navestock, Essex.

Moth Minor G-AFPN in an updated colour scheme taxying at Cranfield, Bedfordshire.

SOURCES

In addition to material available via BAE Systems, and the author's own British Built Aircraft series, the major sources used in creating this work include the following:

Jackson, AJ British Civil Aircraft Since 1919, Putnam

Jackson, AJ De Havilland Aircraft Since 1909, Putnam

McKay, Stuart De Havilland Tiger Moth, Midland Publishing

Ord-Hume, Arthur WJG British Light Aeroplanes – Their Evolution, Development and Perfection 1920 – 1940, GMS Enterprises

Internet resources include:

Malcolm Fillimore's Air Britain files relating to the DH60 and DH80, which can be found at http://www.ab-ix.co.uk/firstfiles.html

and the DH Production List which can be found at http://www.airhistory.org.uk